On This
JOURNEY

A BOOK OF POSITIVITIES

On This

JOURNEY

A BOOK OF POSITIVITIES

IRENE FORD-SMITH

VMH Publishing
Atlanta, GA | New York, NY
www.vmhpublishing.net

Paperback ISBN: 979-8-9865891-4-5

Library of Congress Control Number
Available Upon Request

Published in United States of America
10 9 8 7 6 5 4 3 2 1

ON THIS JOURNEY

On this journey of life, it is woven with twists and turns, hills and valleys, steeps and downhills, ups and downs, tears of sadness, and joy. As I thought about writing my next book, after *Some Glad Morning*, I considered many topics, but this title/thought came to me by way of the Holy Spirit.

What I have learned in my seventy-two years of life are so many lessons I never learned or perhaps were never taught. I grew up in Georgia in a small town called Toccoa. I love my home town for it was a cocoon, a harbor, a place for me to experience life on a smaller scale. Like all small towns of colored folk, I remember downtown having water fountains labeled "white" and "colored." I recall going to Toccoa Clinic with my grandmother, Zemmie Jones, and entering a side door marked "colored," waiting inside a small room for her name to be called. I attended an all-black school, Whitman Street School, with a principal and teachers who loved us, pushed us, and expected the very best of us.

I lived in a colored community, went to a colored Baptist church, Mt. Zion Baptist Church, shopped during the week at "Mr. Roy" groceries where colored folk bought on credit. You simply went to the store with a list provided by your parent and the items were added to the bill. I think back how we never ever purchased something not on the list. We were sent to the store to pick up cigarettes. No one asked about who it was for. Everyone knew it was for your parent. During the week the neighborhood was quiet, children going to school doing homework, and grown folks working. On the weekend, everything changed. There was excitement in the air. The juke joints were jumping, folks were loud from strong drink, and there may be a fight or two.

Sunday morning, it was quiet. I went to church every Sunday although services were only held on the first and third Sunday of the month, but Church School was every Sunday. I loved going to church to hear the deacons pray and sing as they led devotion. I loved going to revivals sitting on the "sinners' bench" until I joined the church. For many years, I didn't quite understand what it meant to "line a hymn." In other words, the deacons would call out the words for you to sing. I just sang "do re mi fa so la ti do" until I learned it was actual words they were saying. I grew up in a one-bedroom home, with a kitchen and bathroom I feared. My sister and I slept in one bed, and my two brothers slept in another bed.

My brothers were always seeing "ghosts" and inevitably in the middle of the night we would be awakened with them screaming of some evil ungodly spirit hovering over them. We would tell them to be quiet; there were no ghost. My sister and I would whisper between us our refusal to look and see. Our mother slept in the living room, and we received our heat from a stove fueled by wood, with kerosene used as an accelerator. I recall visiting my grandmother's home and plopping down in a chair only to jump up screaming and crying. I had accidently sat on an "hot eye" taken from the stovetop. Yes, I received a terrible burn, but it taught me to look before I sat.

My community embraced young people, and their expectation was that we would be more successful than them through education, military, and work. When I graduated from high school, two weeks later I was picked up along with my best friend, Judy, and off to Chattanooga, Tennessee we went to start college in an all-white environment. I cried and cried, unsure and still to this day trying to figure out how my mother made this decision and never discussed it with me, just packed my clothes and off I went with my best friend to integrate a white college. Arriving in Tennessee we cried for several weeks until we ran out of food our parents had packed entering the world of adulthood. It was an adventure.

Yet Jeremiah 29:11 stands up in our hearts **now** but not so much then. I know the plans for you I have you…. Does this mean a loving God allowed me to endure these hardships? My tears, my fears, my trepidation all were working together for my good? On this journey it would have been helpful and uplifting if I had met someone who would have shared this fact. As I look back over my life, I recognize all my friends, family, and others were experiencing life from their personal perspective. Unfortunately, I did not have the foresight or dared to dream of bigger and better. I remember playing "paper dolls" with my siblings, cutting out family figures, clothing, and furniture, setting up an entire household of paper—I was dreaming. I was seeing past my circumstance. On this journey, life lessons are gleamed from every setback, setup, heartbreak, and emotional breakdown.

As you read through Scripture, there is comfort when you look at the lives of those who faced similar difficulties, there are answers for us. David, whose father called all his brothers but him to be considered for the next king, and when the oil would not run, he was summoned. Likewise, Joseph who was born in a blended family, which was totally dysfunctional, and it was hidden within the walls of their home and the hearts of their children. He was hated by his brothers because God gave him a dream. Like Abel whose brother, Cain, despised him because he chose to offer a more excellent sacrifice to God; his brother kills him. Like Abraham looking out for his cousin, Lot, who was selfish. Like Sarah, who commands Hagar to sleep with her husband and bear him a child, and then hates her for it.

As I think about so many children born in neighborhoods whose constant is violence, yet not everyone succumbs to the negative environment. There are those who overcome. Homeless young children, through no fault of their own, have lived at more than twenty addresses while traversing elementary and high school.

Sometimes homeless, sometimes without what are considered basic

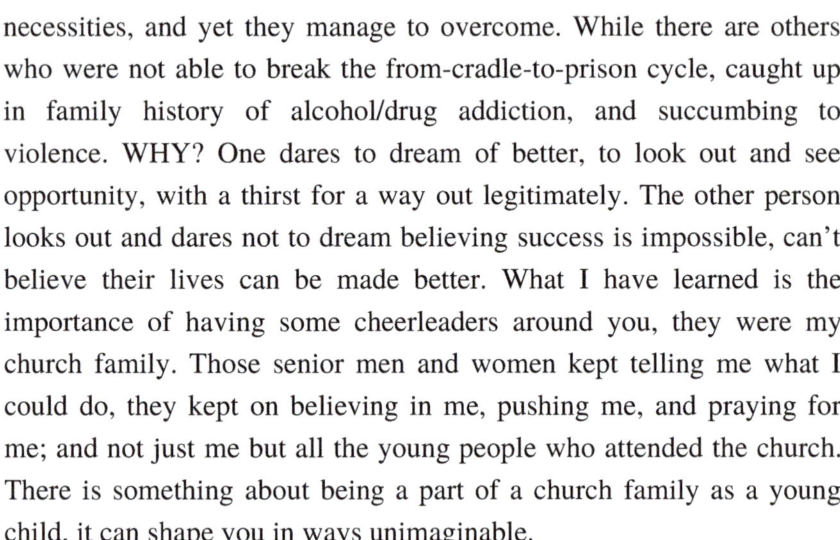

necessities, and yet they manage to overcome. While there are others who were not able to break the from-cradle-to-prison cycle, caught up in family history of alcohol/drug addiction, and succumbing to violence. WHY? One dares to dream of better, to look out and see opportunity, with a thirst for a way out legitimately. The other person looks out and dares not to dream believing success is impossible, can't believe their lives can be made better. What I have learned is the importance of having some cheerleaders around you, they were my church family. Those senior men and women kept telling me what I could do, they kept on believing in me, pushing me, and praying for me; and not just me but all the young people who attended the church. There is something about being a part of a church family as a young child, it can shape you in ways unimaginable.

On this journey of life, we have one thing in common
God loves us!

TIME OF REFLECTION

Do you recall your formative years, what life
lessons did you learn?

Are you holding on to unforgiveness?

What role did attending church/Sunday school
play in your life?

If you could say "thank you" to those family/friends/community leaders who sowed richly and positively into your life, who would they be?

What still brings pain to your heart when you recall?

Leaving the elementary years, high school years and moving into adulthood, at eighteen, nineteen, and twenty, I lived my life as if it were impenetrable, just floating through life. On this journey, as I am older and look back, I realize not only did I waste money but something more precious "time." On this journey, it would have been helpful if I had a little more maturity and seriously understood "days gone, time thrown away" cannot be recaptured. Perhaps it would have changed the way I viewed life or maybe not! Young-adult decisions were made not always from a perspective of looking at my future thirty years down the road instead looking at right now, this weekend. On this journey of life, I've learned as a young adult there were plenty of missteps made.

How much money did I needlessly throw away? How much of my time was wasted? I know this is not everyone's story but those for whom it might be true, it's okay to forgive yourself. For the young person who is reading this book, you have the blessed opportunity to stop and make the turn towards a better financial future. On this journey, I've learned you can't make someone admit their mishaps/missteps until they are ready. On this journey, I learned you can't or shouldn't embarrass or harass someone into doing what is best for them. On this journey, I've learned you must give sound advice, space for the recipient to contemplate what has been shared, and accept their decisions as they face the consequences. In those early years of adulthood, mistakes are made, sometimes life-altering mistakes, but there is a road to recovery if you are willing to do the hard work.

Yes, there are many young people who go to college, join the military, get a great-paying job yet they are miserable! Why? Simply put, they pursued someone else's dream and not theirs. In pursuing your dream, the question must be asked, "How will I finance my living day to day?"

Not depending on someone else to support me. On this journey of life, I've learned those years are a "freeing" time frame where you are just enjoying life. Pursuing your passion means you have to be able to stand up against the naysayers, you have to believer in your dream, and if successful your success impacts everyone around you. Look at the scripture, Daniel, a young man taken captive, refused to eat the food from the King's table, knowing his diet was better. His friends, Shadrach, Meshach, and Abednego were watching Daniel. His refusal, the act of defiance changed the trajectory of everyone else. After Daniel's act of civil disobedience, he was met with success and change the diet for everyone in captivity securing him favor with the King.

As a young woman Esther's obedience changed the outcome for her people; she chose right over wrong. Her life was on the line and God allowed her to see past her current situation. As a young adult, there is little impact saying the decisions you make today will impact your retirement years. Why? Simply because it seems like retirement is light-years away. On this journey, I've learned to motivate a young person to see past the next two weeks is to present a better carrot, one attainable in a shorter period. On this journey of life, I've learned this is an exploring season. We explore smoking cigarettes, alcohol consumption, drugs legal and illegal, pushing limits both legal or illegally, often ignoring the wisdom of family and friends moving as if the sun will shine forever. Fast money, along with fast life if gone unchecked may lead to imprisonment, physically and emotionally.

King David's son, Absalom in his youthful thinking and unchecked anger against his father, slept with his father's wife publicly. Why didn't he have a conversation with his father about his anger? He lacked wisdom. The son of Solomon, Rehoboam, upon death of his father, took bad counsel from his young friends resulting in him losing the kingly reign. The ACLU cites nearly 60,000 youth under the age eighteen are incarcerated in juvenile jails and prisons in the United States (aclu.org).

With the blazing lights of overnight fame using Tik-Tok, the domination of music peddling, "Benjamins" raining, the quest for overnight success young people may be sucked down the drain of promises of fame and fortunes. Is it possible? Yes, but the likelihood of lightning striking career with overnight success is less likely to happen.

It is like the person who spends years trying to win the lottery, instead of pursuing their passion, their dream and making it come to fruition. When you are young, decisions may not have been given the time and consideration needed. Consequences are what we recognize often hours, days, weeks, or years later, which resulted from our decisions or lack thereof. How easy it is to find a reason for our decision: I didn't have anyone to help me, I didn't have sufficient funds, my father/mother were not present in my life, I just didn't know what to do, I was angry, I, I, I…. We can go on forever and ever. At the end of our tirade, we had to accept it was bad decision.

First, we can agree life can be deemed as unfair. We can agree we don't start off on equal grounds or beginnings. We can agree illness, sickness may occur, and all types of setbacks happen in our lives, yet each person is responsible for their decisions. Folks become bitter for a lifetime based on perceived or real instances of hurt/pain from family, friends and/or colleagues. How we respond to these events in our lives is always our decision. There are many persons who have taken the worst scenario, reared in the most violent of neighborhoods, suppressed, oppressed and overcome, while others did not. What can we learn on this journey of life? Decisions can't be rushed; decisions must be viewed with a spirit not steeped in despair!

While there are Hollywood stars, politicians, business entrepreneurs, and professors whose lives illustrate being overcomers of their environment. I think of a young man, who often states, "I don't have to to be a victim of my environment!" which is so true.

This young man spent his formative years in the worst crime-ridden neighborhood in the nation, but he overcame. How? The opportunity presented itself for him to live with his father in a totally different environment. He was moved into his dad's home. Attending a new high school, he had a choice to make—get in the game or reject the opportunity! He chose wisely, and later recognized as having a brilliant mind. Attending high school, you tend not to be concerned or give thought to your classmates' environment, unaware of the hellish environment your classmate might be living. **Choices cannot be overlooked or dismissed.** Thus, we have to be careful of how we compare our lives to someone else. 1 Timothy 4:12 reads "Let no man despise thy youth; but be thou an example of the believers, in word, in conversation, in charity, in spirit, in faith, in purity." (King James Version) But what if you are not yet a believer? First, the scripture admonishes parents (Ephesians 6:4) "do not provoke your children to anger but bring them up in the discipline and instruction of the Lord."

Every person who calls themselves a Christian has a responsibility to pray for children who are lost, to pray for their salvation, to walk upright before them, to be ready always to encourage them in the ways of the Lord. It is not easy because youth will outwardly reject the truth but inwardly, I believe, the seed of success has been sown. Sadly, on this journey, I have learned some youth will reject all you have to offer, will curse you, will not receive anything you have to say. It is a reality. What can you do? Keep praying for them, and as opportunity presents itself, continue to point them in the right direction.

TIME OF REFLECTION

Do you recall some of the wrong decisions you
made as a young person?

When you consider your family and friends,
have you taken the time to pray for them?

As opportunity presents itself, have you taken the time to listen to the dreams of a young person and offer constructive remarks to achieve their dream?

Are you a dream chaser or a dream dasher?

As a mature adult, do you have a desire to sow
into the lives of young adults?

Money, money, money, got to have it—entering the world of work. No plans really, just get a car, my own place, and enjoy life. I got a job, purchased a car, got an apartment, and I enjoyed life. On this journey looking back, I can see the money I burned up, blew up, threw up, and gave up. When you are young, serious savings, serious investments are not always at the top of your list. I am thankful this mindset has changed for some young people; they have goals with plans of retiring at age thirty-five. Sounds frivolous, impossible, but I say to them "why not?" If there is an opportunity to change the trajectory of your life, it is when you are young and have the opportunity to perhaps dictate your financial future. On this journey, I have learned when you are young, just starting to work, it seems like light-years before you will be old like fifty. And thinking of purchasing long-term health care insurance, life insurance, or any other commodity is not something you concern yourself with.

On this journey, I have learned to share with younger persons in their twenties, thirties, forties, and fifties advice they will appreciate in years yet to come. We oftentimes graduate from high school, colleges, universities, and the military with no classes on financial management, or life in general. We are not taught how to handle rejections (rejected for a job, rejected for a loan, rejected by someone you wanted to kindle a relationship.) It is after experiencing these rejections I have learned to ask myself these questions: (1) Was I properly prepared for the job; (2) Was this the right purpose for me and (3) Was I good steward over my finances. On this journey I have learned rejection made me stronger, the rejection made me take the appropriate steps to improve my credit, my thoughts towards money, and the rejection simply meant that the person was not the right one at that point in my life.

On this journey, I have learned we can be impulsive without thought of the repercussions—as a famous shoemaker states "just do it!"

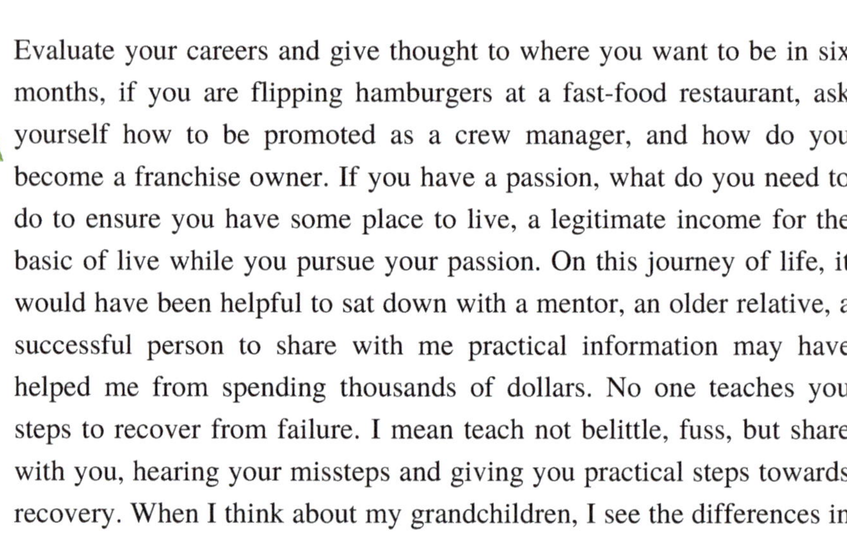

Evaluate your careers and give thought to where you want to be in six months, if you are flipping hamburgers at a fast-food restaurant, ask yourself how to be promoted as a crew manager, and how do you become a franchise owner. If you have a passion, what do you need to do to ensure you have some place to live, a legitimate income for the basic of live while you pursue your passion. On this journey of life, it would have been helpful to sat down with a mentor, an older relative, a successful person to share with me practical information may have helped me from spending thousands of dollars. No one teaches you steps to recover from failure. I mean teach not belittle, fuss, but share with you, hearing your missteps and giving you practical steps towards recovery. When I think about my grandchildren, I see the differences in how each of them when views money. Some work very hard, two jobs, plus high school and college to support themselves and others you just hate to answer the telephone because their hand is always out.

Some mistakes I made along the way and now I'm learning how to say "NO" I don't have money to loan or give. Give this book to a younger person and share together this chapter and lessons to be learned and implemented immediately. I think about the Prodigal Son returning home. After making every misstep possible, he returned broke and humbled, willing to serve as a slave for his father. His father could react in a number of ways, and we are blown away by his response. He called for the servants to begin preparation for a party to return his son to his position in the family and welcomed him in love. WOW! Talking about falling down and your family receiving you in love. The Scripture provides no additional information on the son's failures, leaving us with him learning his lesson and being restored.

On this journey of life, I have met people who are reliving "past hurts" and regurgitate the story over and over. Pain inflicted early in life leaves a mark, positive or negative on your soul. While some folks can grow from it, others can't let go or refuse to let go of their ain. Oftentimes spending money makes them feel better but can create other problems.

On this journey of life, I have met people who are reliving "past hurts" and regurgitate the story over and over. Pain inflicted early in life leaves a mark, positive or negative on your soul. While some folks can grow from it, others can't let go or refuse to let go of their pain. Oftentimes spending money makes them feel better but can create other problems.

TIME OF REFLECTION

Thinking about your early years, as a young person what life lessons did you learn about money?

Thinking about you save, spend, set goals in your finances, what changes, if any, do you need to make going forward.

Thinking about your children, family members, or friends who are younger, write a letter of financial encouragement based on your life experiences.

Looking back over your life, what experiences make you grateful?

Sex, marriage, and divorce are topics difficult to discuss openly for some. On this journey of life, sex was not openly discussed in my home; it just wasn't. Neither do I remember hearing a lot about in the classroom. My friends and I never talked about whether or not we were having sex. To be quite honest, I never thought of asking. On this journey, I have learned be mindful of who you decide to lose your virginity with or with whom you share intimacy. On this journey of life, I have learned the sexual connection means more to women than men. I know in this age where promiscuity is not even thought of as before, I do believe both boy/man, girl/woman need to think about their own body and their own mental dynamics when it comes to sex. Conquering a mass number of men/women at the end of the days means absolutely nothing when you can lay down and not be emotionally attached to a person.

On this journey, open sex is not new neither are the ramifications; although it may never be told, many hearts have been broken trying to create intimate relationships from a one-sided encounter. It is commonplace to hear about a man who has several children by multiple women in our community. What are the dynamics of this type of relationship? The children may suffer from (1) not having a brotherly/sisterly relationship with their biological sister/brother; (2) the mothers may suffer from not having a thriving relationship where she and children are first; and (3) the father as much as he may try, a child may experience feelings of abandonment and neglect. Yes, these things may occur even with married couples, but the disruption from other mothers/fathers is not a factor.

On this journey of life, I asked myself "how do you explain to your child several brothers/sisters with several different women?" On this journey of life, it may not seem important, something you can get past, but when those children grow up understanding they share birthdays with a sibling from another woman/man, they share the same father/mother with others, quality time with each child may be negatively impacted, and blending them as a family unit as early as possible is critical to foster healthy understandings of their particular family blend and themselves.

On this journey of life sexual intimacy has changed. It's relevancy in a relationship is not always based on a serious relationship between two people. On this journey of life, it's troubling at times for me to see the promotion of plural relationships no matter whether it is agreed or not. I say "or not" as there are plural relationships on one side and not on the other. On this journey of life, I shake my head in disbelief as I see young women "turn up" at concerts exposing themselves on stage, off stage, in lewd acts that demean their status. On this journey of life, I can't believe the success people experience from making and sharing sex tapes of their intimate moments. On this journey of life, I wonder what emotional turmoil, if any, will trouble the spirits of these young people as they move into emotional and physical maturity.

On this journey of life, sex has been used as an emotional tool, as a "bond" to hold two people together; it will fizzle out. Sex has been used as an emotional tool creating bondages and a false perspective on your value. Sex has been used as the true essence of "love!" It is not! When we begin to talk about sexual intimacy, the conversation must be elevated from just two people coming together for a "booty call." Sexual intimacy is not created overnight, intimacy starts before the bedroom, getting to know the person likes, dislikes, dreams, passions, hopes, fears, goals, with the creation of a friendship which grows into love (with respect) and boundaries with each other.

Sexual intimacy in Scripture is referred to in Genesis 2:24–25 "Therefore a man shall leave his father and his mother and hold fast to his wife, and they shall become one flesh.

And the man and his wife were both naked and were not embarrassed or ashamed in each other's presence." Again, in Hebrews 13:4, "Marriage is honorable among all, and the bed undefiled; but fornicators and adulterers God will judge." In the book of Proverbs 5:15–20 (Ampc) reads "Drink waters out of your own cistern, and fresh running waters out of your own well. Should your offspring be dispersed abroad as water brooks in the streets? Let our children be for you alone, and not the children of strangers with you. Let your fountain be blessed and rejoice in the wife of your youth. Let her be as the loving hind and pleasant doe—let her bosom satisfy you at all times, and always be transported with delight in her love. Why should you, my son, be infatuated with a loose woman, embrace the bosom of an outsider, and go astray?"

The Bible speaks about the responsibility of husband and wife to each other. 1 Corinthians 7:3–5 (Ampc) The husband should give to his wife her conjugal rights, and likewise the wife to her husband…Do not refuse and deprive and defraud each other, except perhaps by mutual consent for a time, so that you may devote yourselves unhindered to prayer. But afterwards resume marital relations, lest Satan temp you through your lack of restraint of sexual desire." Lovemaking is natural in a marital relationship. Lovemaking is beautiful and should be shared only with someone who is ready to make a long-term commitment to you. What I have learned on this road of life having been divorced, having experienced love, I am thankful I learned my value. I learned through mistakes, I learned through my own acts of impulsiveness, I learned through being loved and accepted with all my frailties.

Lovemaking is intimate and while there are marriages called "open," I can't accept this kind of relationship. On this journey called life, each person has to make their own personal decision on what they will or will not accept in their marriage, and it does not matter what others think or believe.

On this journey called life, I have learned the Scripture from a child, but I did not always live by God's Word resulting in it costing me some personal joy, peace, and putting bumps on the roads I travelled. The marital vows must be considered as a binding contract with your spouse and God. Yes, I know contracts can be broken; after all, I am divorced. However, before you say "I do" take the time to read the vows and understand the lifetime commitment you are making to another person. Are you willing to love them in good times and bad, when they falter, make mistakes, commit infidelity, asking for forgiveness? Are you willing to love them for richer or poorer, when the money and security is not present are you willing to remain committed to that person until your circumstance's change to a positive? Are you willing to stand by the person side when they become ill, when they become incompetent, don't know their name, can't take care of the basic of living for themselves, will you be willing to love them in the midst of these life issues? Are you willing to keep your commitment to only commit yourself to them and none other? The binding contract is real and must not be taken likely, for you end it commitment until death do us part!

It took a while for me to move forward after divorce. I was stuck in believing I could never remarry. My first husband committed infidelity, and to be quite honest, we should never have married. Love can be a beautiful symphony or a beast which pushes you, drives you to some unexpected lows, drives you to some emotion reactions you never dreamed possible for yourself, and may even drive a wedge between you and those who want the best for you.

On this journey called life, I have learned to ask yourself "what are my deal-breakers?" and stay with it. I have learned on this journey called life, don't accept anyone treating you less than the person God created you to be. Don't ever accept someone putting their hands on you and calling it love or blaming you for their actions. Don't ever accept someone cussing you, calling you every derogatory name they can think of and blame you for their response.

Don't ever accept anyone denying you a relationship with your family. Don't ever accept someone denying your value, someone saying disparaging remarks against you or your family, and wanting you to believe their word is gospel truth. Don't ever a cheater, a serial liar, a person who have no desire to do better, they drain you, they take away from you. I have learned on this journey called life, I am worthy of being treated as a queen, I am worthy of being honored, I am worthy of love, honor, and respect, and I must be willing to give the same.

Divorce! I hate the word it conjures up past hurt and pain. Divorce is a separation, an ending of dreams once shared. Divorce ends a chapter and begins a new one! I was shattered after my divorce, I was angry, I was bewildered, I just wasn't able yet to put the pieces together to understand all that had transpired. Love is not a water faucet you turn on and off but it is fluid, divorce stamped on a paper does not end your love for the person. If children are involved, divorce does not mean we no longer have to interact. On this journey called life, I've learned when the person asked for a divorce give it to them. You can't make someone love you. Yes, you can fight for your marriage but if the other person is not trying to remain in the marriage it may be futile. Giving in to the other person demands for a divorce, does not mean God can't bring the two of you back together again. Don't ever say "I don't want anything!" There is community property, community savings, community building and should be equitably divided.

Once divorce, be mindful of how you hit the dating scene. Keep your wit about you, don't allow your hurt emotions to drive you into the arms or situations of wrong people. Don't adopt the mindset of "I just want a man/woman!" Take time to grieve your loss, take time to sort through your emotions, and don't become a stalker.

Start a journal of do's and don'ts moving forward, ask yourself going forward how can I better communicate through listening and expressing emotions. Don't allow your emotions to hurt or kill someone because they say there is no longer any love present. Rather, value yourself understanding you will love again it is not the end. Where children are present, stay away from negative commentary about the divorcing parent. Communicate to the children they are still the priority of both parents. Don't bring your dates around your children. Judge the actions of the person you are dating, how do they communicate, how do they handle their frustration and anger, how do they interact with their children, children's mother, family, and friends.

Learn to listen to the inner voice, the Holy Spirit, telling you to walk away. When considering remarriage, spend time to know the person. Don't start any behavior or accept any behavior contrary to your beliefs. Pray and seek God's face.

TIME OF REFLECTION

What are your must haves and deal breakers in a relationship? What is your love language, and how do you communicate it to your significant person?

If you are divorced, make a list of what you perceived
went wrong. What did you learn about yourself from the
divorce?

As you begin to date, what are the pitfalls you need to avoid? As you interact in social settings, how quickly do you tell your love story of being divorced? Do you view prospective dates as "just like my former spouse?"

ON THIS JOURNEY OF LIFE.
WE HAVE ONE THING IN COMMON
GOD LOVES US!